CALLIGRAPHY

Caroline Young

Designed by Jane Felstead

Consultant: Susan Hufton
(Fellow of the Society of Scribes)

Contents

Illustrated by Chris Lyon and Paul Sullivan
Calligraphy by Susan Hufton

Additional calligraphy by Solos Solou
When you see the symbol ✝, ask an adult for help.

WHAT IS CALLIGRAPHY?

Calligraphy is the art of beautiful writing. The basic techniques of the calligrapher are the same today as they were centuries ago. Here you can see the development of calligraphy from the earliest forms of writing. You will find out how to write some of the calligraphy styles shown here later in this book.

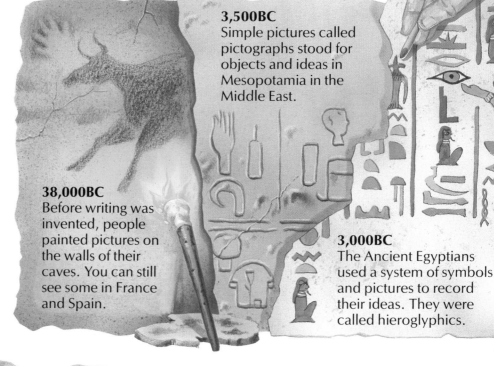

38,000BC
Before writing was invented, people painted pictures on the walls of their caves. You can still see some in France and Spain.

3,500BC
Simple pictures called pictographs stood for objects and ideas in Mesopotamia in the Middle East.

3,000BC
The Ancient Egyptians used a system of symbols and pictures to record their ideas. They were called hieroglyphics.

1st century AD
The Ancient Romans adapted the Greeks' alphabet to produce their own 23 capital letters (see page 8). They carved, or incised, them into stone and marble.

The Romans used a broad nib, held at a constant angle, to write in books. This made simpler capitals, called Rustics. These were the first calligraphy letters.

Rustic capitals

1st to 10th centuries AD
In some countries, the letters J, U and W were added to the 23 Roman capitals to make a 26 letter alphabet.

JU W

Uncials

Around the 6th century, monks used a calligraphy style called Uncials to write beautifully decorated religious books. You can learn how to write Uncials on page 12.

SICUT NOUIT ME PATER
ET EGO AGNOSCO PATREM
ET ANIMAM MEAM PONO
PRO OMNIB...

Versal

Adquem autem angel
adextris meis quoadu
scabellum pedum tu
amm.

Carolingian minuscules

By the 9th century, most people were using small letters, or minuscules, as well as capitals. The most common style was called the Carolingian minuscule (see page 40).

Capital letters built up with several pen strokes were often used with minuscules. They were called Versals (see page 20).

2,500BC

The first real writing, called cuneiform, was invented in Mesopotamia. Marks made in clay with a wedge-shaped tool stood for sounds. These made up words.

1,500BC

At this time, the Chinese began using a complicated script with more than 1500 characters. Each character stood for a whole idea. You can find out how to write some on page 27.

1,000BC

Sea-traders called Phoenicians used an alphabet of 22 letters. They spread this alphabet to many Mediterranean countries.

500BC

The Ancient Greeks adapted some of the Phoenician alphabet and added some vowels (A,E,I and O) as well.

13th-15th century AD

To fit more onto a line, people started writing narrower letters closer together. This gradually developed into the Gothic style you can see on page 16.

Tunc det ei eps uungam pac tozalem dicens.

Around the end of the 1400s, people wanted a writing style that was simpler than Gothic. Scholars in Italy developed Italics, which could be beautiful calligraphy or just elegant handwriting (see pages 18-19).

Italic handwriting
↓

Signor, che parti et tempri gli elementi,

15th-19th century AD

In 1450, the first printing press was set up in Germany. Its letters were based on the Gothic calligraphy style.

und vorcht scheide vo euch nirht ivo ir wandett·wi

↑
Gothic print

Once books were printed and not written by hand, calligraphy became less important. People just used beautiful writing for their everyday handwriting.

Wilhelmse

Today

Around 1900, the scholar Edward Johnston revived the art of calligraphy. He taught historical styles and one he developed himself based on a 10th century manuscript. It was called Foundational.

10th century letters
↓

angeli
angels

↑
Foundational letters

Calligraphy is not easy, so don't worry if your first attempts are not very good. As you go through this book, try writing as many styles as you can.

3

STARTING OUT

Below is the basic equipment you need to start doing calligraphy. You can try the main techniques using the simple things on page 5. There are details about buying proper calligraphy pens and nibs on page 6.

Basic equipment

You can buy all these things from a good art supply store.

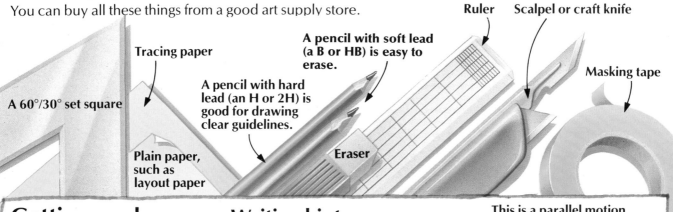

Tracing paper

A 60°/30° set square

A pencil with hard lead (an H or 2H) is good for drawing clear guidelines.

A pencil with soft lead (a B or HB) is easy to erase.

Plain paper, such as layout paper

Eraser

Ruler

Scalpel or craft knife

Masking tape

Getting ready

Most calligraphers prefer to write on a sloping surface, such as a drawing board. Writing on a flat surface can make the ink flood out of your pen.

Try sticking a sheet of paper to the back of a tray. Rest one edge of a tray on your knees and lean the other against the edge of a table.

Lean a board against a pile of heavy books on a table for a more stable writing surface.

You could make a drawing board from a piece of wood from around your home, or plywood from a lumber yard. It should be at least 2 feet long, 1½ feet wide and ½ inch thick.

Writing hints

Here are some hints to help you produce better calligraphy.

- Sit near a window if possible. If you need a desk lamp, it should shine over the opposite shoulder to your writing hand.

- Tape several sheets of paper under the sheet you are going to write on. They will act as a pad.

- Tape another sheet of paper over your work to keep it clean. Move your worksheet up to start each new line.

- Sit up straight, with both feet flat on the floor as shown in the picture on the right. Keep the part of your arm from your wrist to your elbow on the board as you write.

This is a parallel motion drawing board. Many professional calligraphers use them, but they are very expensive. A home-made board is fine to start with.

Paper for padding

Worksheet

Paper to keep your work clean.

The correct angle

Calligraphers write with a broad nib held at a constant angle. In this book, pictures like the one on the right show you the angle to hold your nib at as you write each calligraphy style.

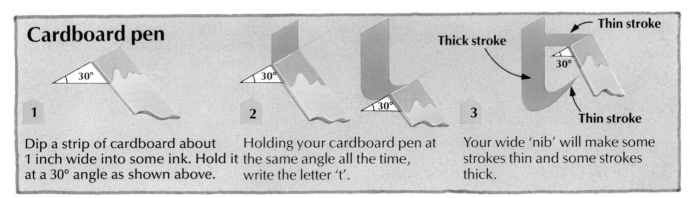

Hold your nib at the angle shown here.

30°

It will look like this.

Thick and thin

When you write like this with a broad nib, you will find that your pen makes thick and thin strokes. Try it yourself using one of the simple broad-nibbed 'pens' shown here.

Cardboard pen

30° **1**

30° **2**

Thick stroke

Thin stroke

30° **3**

Thin stroke

1 Dip a strip of cardboard about 1 inch wide into some ink. Hold it at a 30° angle as shown above.

2 Holding your cardboard pen at the same angle all the time, write the letter 't'.

3 Your wide 'nib' will make some strokes thin and some strokes thick.

Tip

The 'pens' on this page were made from the things shown below. Another inexpensive way of getting used to how a broad-edged nib makes letters is to buy a calligraphy felt-tip pen. Many art shops sell them.

A wax crayon

Strips of cardboard

Ink (Non-waterproof is best. It will not clog your pen.)

Pieces of felt

Felt pens

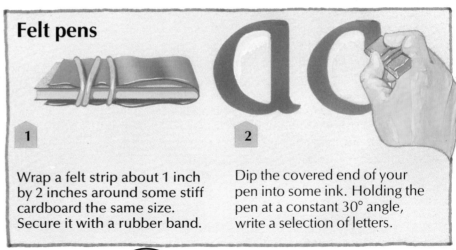

1 Wrap a felt strip about 1 inch by 2 inches around some stiff cardboard the same size. Secure it with a rubber band.

2 Dip the covered end of your pen into some ink. Holding the pen at a constant 30° angle, write a selection of letters.

Wax crayon

1 Rub a piece of wax crayon until one side is flattened. This makes your broad writing-edge.

2 Hold the crayon between your thumb and forefinger at a 30° angle and write any word.

Pens and Nibs

Most calligraphy is written with an ink-filled pen. Your pen is the most important piece of equipment you will buy. Here you can find out what sorts of pens are available, to help you choose.

Choosing your pen

There are two types of calligraphy pen. They are dip pens and fountain pens with calligraphy nibs.

Dip pens

Dip pens have three parts: a nib, a pen-holder and a reservoir to hold ink. Each part is inexpensive to buy and easy to replace or change. You may have to go to an art shop to get one.

Nibs are available in ten different widths. The widest, marked 0 or 1, are best to start with. If you are left-handed, you will need a nib called a left oblique nib.

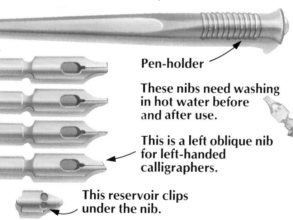

Pen-holder

These nibs need washing in hot water before and after use.

This is a left oblique nib for left-handed calligraphers.

This reservoir clips under the nib.

Fountain pens

Fountain pens have a supply of ink inside the pen. They are either refilled with ink from a bottle or with replaceable cartridges.

Many art shops sell fountain pens with wide nibs for calligraphy. It is expensive to replace broken nibs and the nib sizes available can be limited, however.

Assembling a dip pen

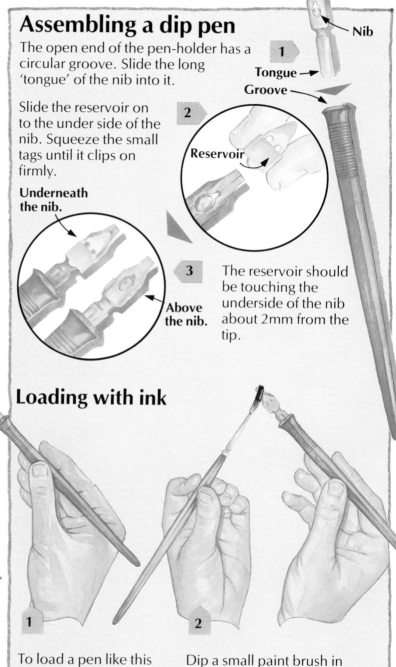

The open end of the pen-holder has a circular groove. Slide the long 'tongue' of the nib into it.

1

Nib

Tongue

Groove

Slide the reservoir on to the under side of the nib. Squeeze the small tags until it clips on firmly.

2

Reservoir

Underneath the nib.

3

Above the nib.

The reservoir should be touching the underside of the nib about 2mm from the tip.

Loading with ink

1

To load a pen like this one, turn it so that the reservoir is facing upwards. Hold it so that the nib end of the pen-holder is higher.

2

Dip a small paint brush in ink*. Gently wipe the ink onto the nib by moving the brush downwards. Repeat this until the ink flows into the reservoir.

6

Remember to use non-waterproof ink

Writing with your pen

You might find writing with an ink-filled calligraphy pen takes some practice. To get started, make each of the pen-stroke patterns shown below. Follow the arrows and try to keep your pen angle constant as you write.

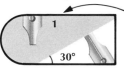

This number tells you what size nib to use.

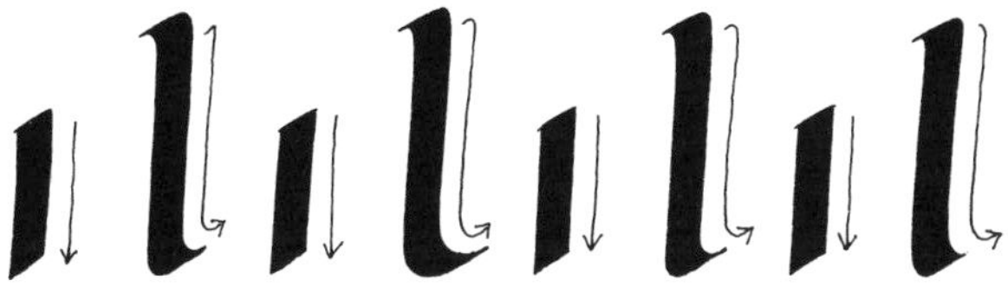

Take the nib off the page between these strokes.

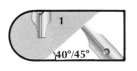  

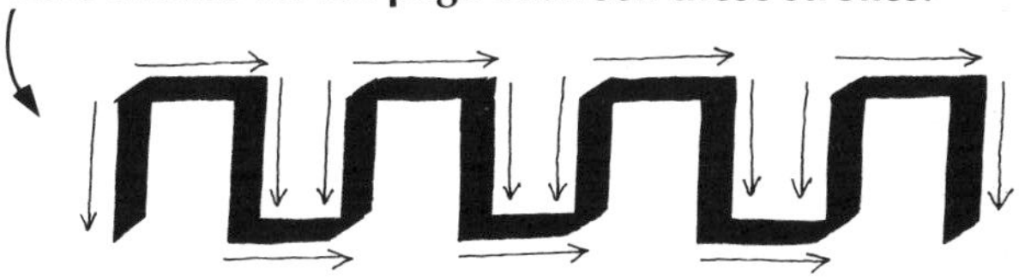

This time, take the nib off the page and draw the second stroke towards you.

Making letters

Calligraphy letters are not written with one continuous pen stroke, like ordinary handwriting. They are made up of several strokes and you take the pen off the paper between them.

Here, two curved strokes make a letter 'O'.

This 'S' is made up of three different strokes.

This calligraphy 'W' has four separate strokes.

You will find out exactly how every letter in the alphabet is formed in each calligraphy style on the pages ahead.

Pen problems

Here are some of the problems you may come across when you first start writing with a calligraphy pen. Possible solutions to them are shown here, too.

Ink is not flowing
- Wash the nib in hot water, it could be greasy. Dry it with a tissue.
- Check the reservoir tabs are not too tight.

Ink is blobby
- Check that the ink has flowed into the reservoir.
- See if the reservoir is too far from the nib.

Strokes are ragged
- Check that the full width of nib is making contact with the paper.

Split strokes
- Make sure you are not pressing too hard, forcing the two parts of the nib to splay apart.

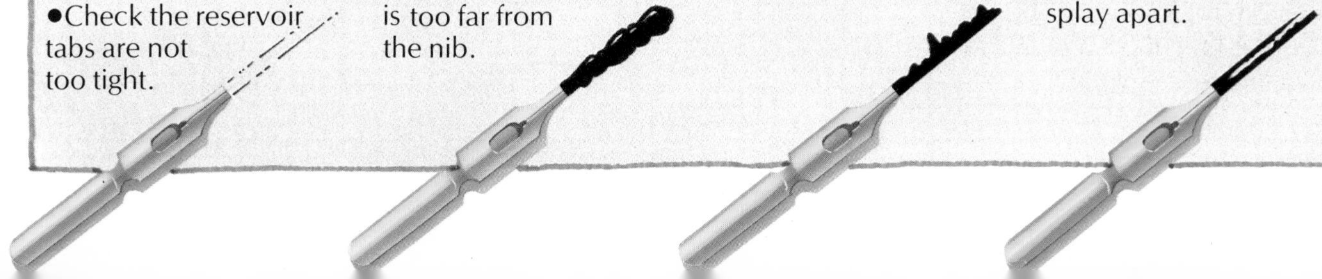

CAPITAL LETTERS

The 26 letters used in most Western languages are called roman letters. They can be written in many different styles. Their basic shapes are adapted from 23 capital letters, or majuscules, used by the Ancient Romans (see page 2). Small letters, or minuscules, developed several centuries later.

Skeleton capitals

The capital letters the Romans used were all based on a grid. They were also divided into groups of letters with similar shapes.

Here you can see them in their groups. They are shown in their simplest form, called a skeleton.

How to write them

1 Fit a medium nib, such as a 3½, into your calligraphy pen and load it with ink. Try some of the practice strokes from page 9 to 'warm up'.

2 Put tracing paper over each grid, one at a time. Make the strokes of each skeleton letter, following the direction of the arrows.

Checkpoints

•Remember to take your pen off the paper between strokes.

•Check the pen angle of each letter before you start.

•Check that your finished letters look like those on page 40.

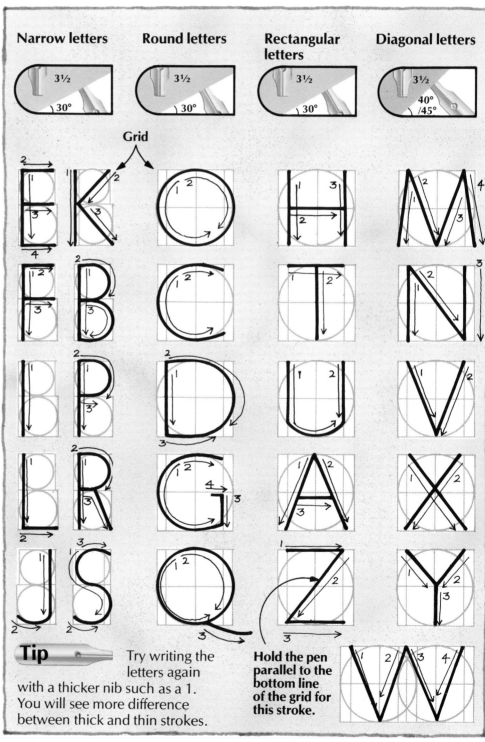

Narrow letters 3½ 30°

Round letters 3½ 30°

Rectangular letters 3½ 30°

Diagonal letters 3½ 40° /45°

Grid

Tip Try writing the letters again with a thicker nib such as a 1. You will see more difference between thick and thin strokes.

Hold the pen parallel to the bottom line of the grid for this stroke.

Straight lines

It is easier to write calligraphy between two parallel pencil guidelines. To make sure they start straight, align side A of your set square with the edge of your paper. as shown on the right. Draw a pencil line along side B. Move your set square down and draw another guideline. Use your ruler to lengthen them.

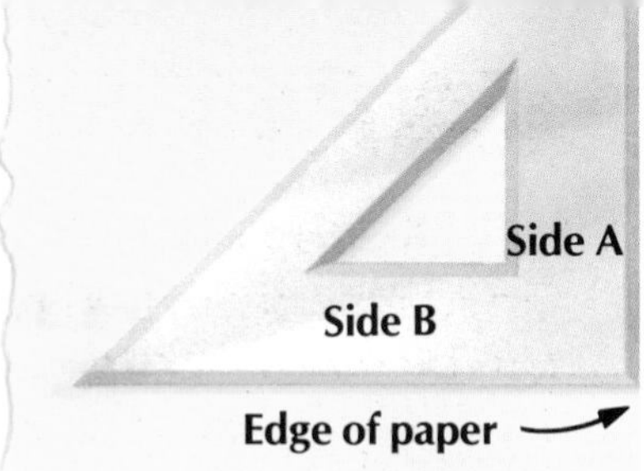

Side A

Side B

Edge of paper ➛

Check your spacing

1 It is important to leave an even amount of space between letters in calligraphy. Rule enough pairs of lines ½ inch apart to write your name and address. Leave ⅕ inch between each pair.

2 Using the nib size and pen angles on page 8, write your name and address between the guidelines. Try and keep an equal space between letters.

3 Lightly shade in the area between letters with a pencil. Stand back and see whether the shaded areas look roughly the same size. With practice, you should be able to judge the right spacing just by looking.

Leave more space between two letters with vertical strokes.

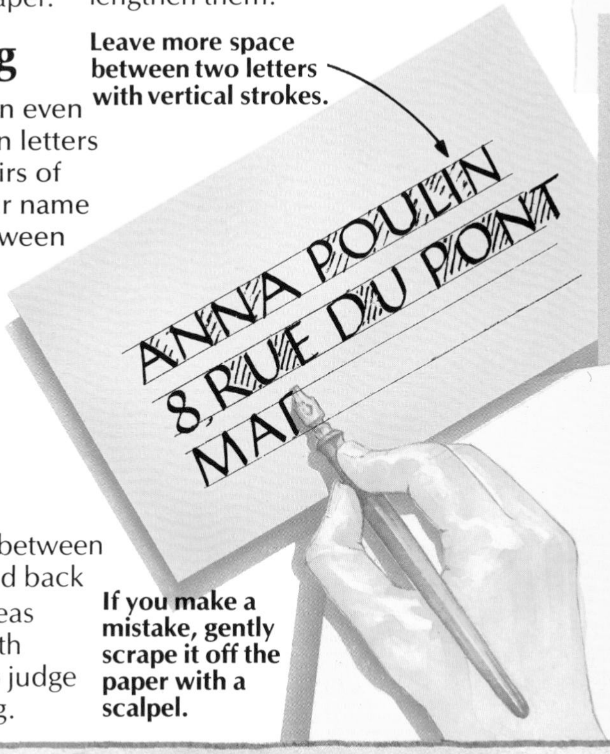

ANNA POULIN
8, RUE DU PONT
MAI

If you make a mistake, gently scrape it off the paper with a scalpel.

Capital calligraphy

When you feel ready, try using Roman capitals for a special piece of work. You could buy a greeting card with no message inside it and write your own.

GOOD LUCK
love
Maria

Serifs

The picture below shows some letters carved into stone by the Ancient Romans. The decorative 'feet' on the end of the letter strokes are called serifs.

In stone, they were formed by the mason's chisel. In calligraphy, serifs can either be built into the pen stroke or added on afterwards.

This serif is a small hook before the stroke.

These serifs are straight strokes added onto the letter.

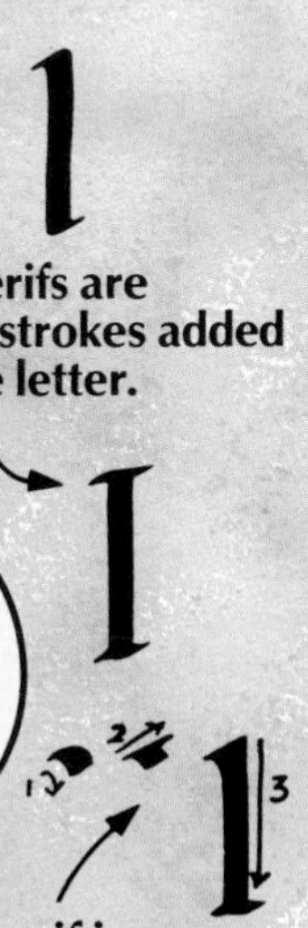

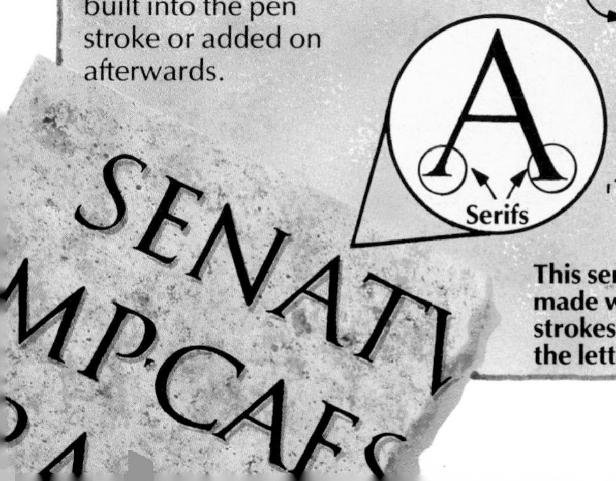

A Serifs

This serif is made with two strokes before the letter stroke.

Sans serif

Letters that do not have serifs are called sans serif. This means 'without serif' in French.

With your calligraphy pen, write the same word three times.

Now try adding a different sort of serif to the letters of each word. Stand back, and see how different the letters look.

ROM

ROM

ROM

Tip Once you feel confident about writing these letters, try adding serifs as you write each one. This might take some practice.

SENATV
MP.CAES

Minuscules

Here you can find out how small letters, or minuscules, are formed in calligraphy. They can be written in many different styles. Once you have learned some basic facts about them, you should be able to master any calligraphy style.

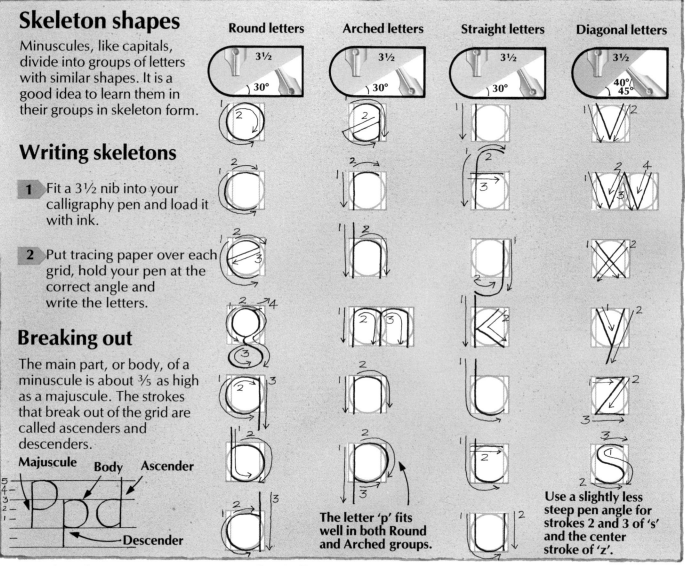

Skeleton shapes

Minuscules, like capitals, divide into groups of letters with similar shapes. It is a good idea to learn them in their groups in skeleton form.

Round letters · **Arched letters** · **Straight letters** · **Diagonal letters**

Writing skeletons

1 Fit a 3½ nib into your calligraphy pen and load it with ink.

2 Put tracing paper over each grid, hold your pen at the correct angle and write the letters.

Breaking out

The main part, or body, of a minuscule is about ⅗ as high as a majuscule. The strokes that break out of the grid are called ascenders and descenders.

Majuscule · Body · Ascender · Descender

The letter 'p' fits well in both Round and Arched groups.

Use a slightly less steep pen angle for strokes 2 and 3 of 's' and the center stroke of 'z'.

Basic shape

All Gothic letters (see page 16) have straight sides, like this 'o'.

All minuscules in one calligraphy style usually relate to the letter 'o'. It is called the basic shape. It is shown each time you learn a new style in this book.

x-height

The height of the body of a minuscule is called its x-height. It is calculated in nib widths, made by holding your nib like this and making a short mark.

How high?

This x-height is 4 nib widths.

A picture like this shows you how high to make all the minuscules in this book. Ascenders and descenders are about ½ as long as the x-height.

Ruling up

If you are writing minuscules in calligraphy, you need to draw pencil guidelines their x-height apart. This is called ruling up.

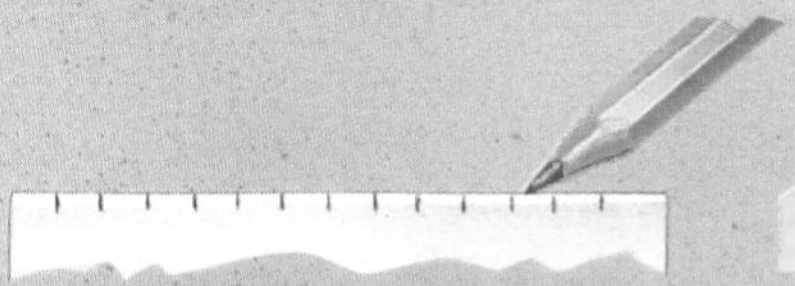

1 Use your set square and ruler to draw a straight line across your paper, as shown at the top of page 9.

2 Make the right number of nib widths for the x-height on the left-hand margin. See how to do this on page 10.

3 Rule a second line at the top of the x-height. Use your set square to start it if you need to.

The Foundational alphabet

This style, called Foundational, is closely based on the skeleton minuscules on page 9.

Below are the x-height and basic shape. Rule up, then try to copy the letters. Use the same pen angles as for the skeletons.

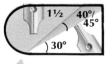

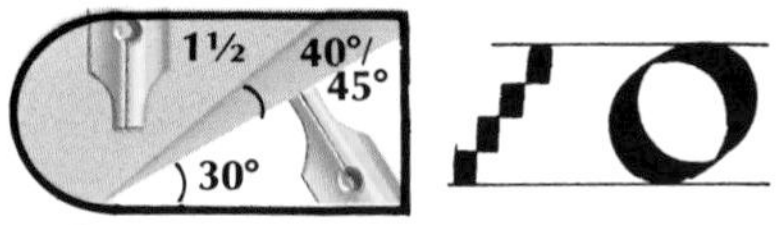

Checkpoints

- Stand back from your letters. Check that the spaces inside the round and arched letters look the same size.

- Check that your letters do not slope backwards. Use your set square to draw some straight vertical pencil lines through your writing line to guide you.

A calligraphy bookmark

Foundational letters are quite clear and simple, so they are useful for all sorts of purposes.

Try writing out a favorite saying or poem in Foundational letters. You could write it on a strip of colored cardboard to make a bookmark, like the one shown here.

You can use the capitals on page 9 with Foundational letters. Make them 6 nib widths high.

Leave the width of a small 'o' between words.

Leave twice the x-height between lines of writing, as shown here.

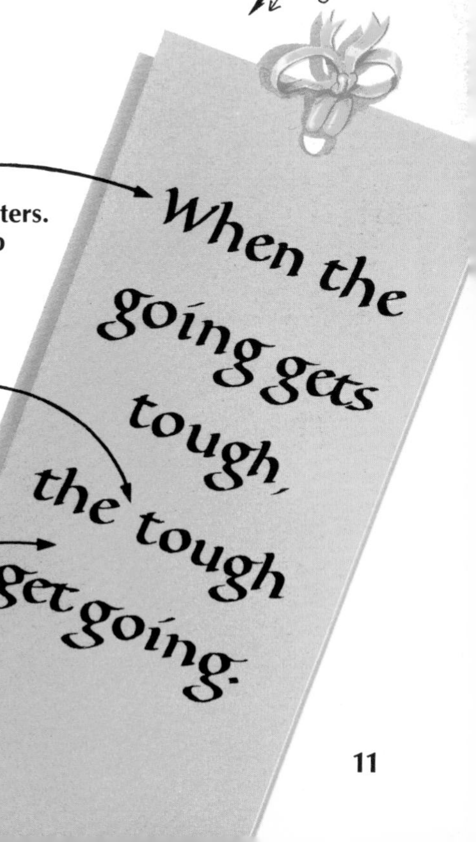

When the going gets tough, the tough get going.

The Look of Letters

The style and size of any calligraphy letters you write will make a powerful impression on your reader. Once you know a variety of styles, you can decide which one is best for each piece of work. The calligraphy letters shown on this page, called Uncials, are ideal for trying out different effects.

Uncials

Uncials were used from the 4th century forward. Although some Uncials had ascenders and descenders, they were not proper minuscules. These developed later.

Rule up a piece of paper using the x-height shown below. Then carefully copy the Uncial alphabet, following the arrows. Keep practicing until your letters look like those on the right.

This x-height is 3½ nib widths.

1½

15° 20°

Use a 20° pen angle to write 'v','w','x' and 'y'.

Family tree

Uncials have a historical 'feel', so you could use them to write out your family tree. Try starting with yourself and working back through your family as far as you can. First, find out who married whom and if they had children. There are numbers on page 46 you could use for dates.

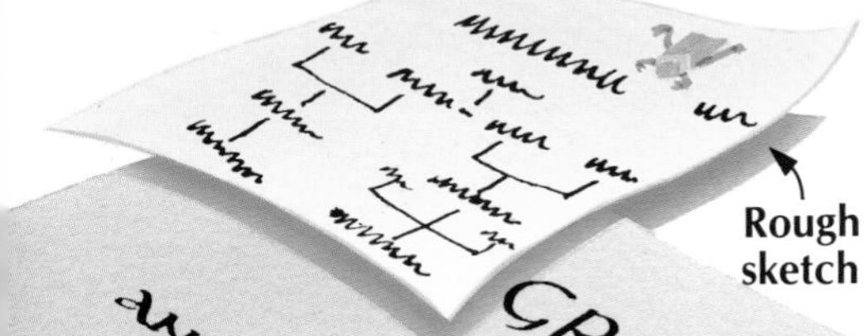

Rough sketch

GREY FAMILY

ANN
PAUL m. ELSA
1932
AMY
JAMES m. NICOLA
1967
JOHN
PETER m. LISA
1929
CHRIS
JOE
ALBERT m. EMMA
1897
WILL

You could invent a family 'symbol' or crest.

You could stick photographs of people next to their names on your tree.

1 Make a small rough sketch of your family tree. This will show you how much space it takes up on the page.

2 Draw the lines or 'branches' of your tree on your writing paper. Rule up writing guidelines where you will need to fill in names.

3 Write your family's names in Uncials. Write larger letters for capitals.

4 Go over the lines of the tree using a ruler and a felt-tip pen so that they are clear and crisp.

5 Erase your writing guidelines carefully.

Letter weight

You can alter the impression a letter makes in two simple ways. You can write it with a different nib, or change its x-height. This affects what is called the letter's 'weight', (how dark or light it looks). There are examples of different weights of calligraphy letters below.

Tip

Try out a selection of nibs and letter heights when you are planning a piece of calligraphy.

Changing the nib

alphabet

alphabet

These words are the same x-height but they were written with different nibs. The second word, written with a thicker nib, looks darker and is longer.

heavy writing is dark, clear and strong

Changing the x-height

alphabet

alphabet

These words were written with the same nib, but have different x-heights. The first word looks much denser or heavier and takes up less space.

LIGHTWEIGHT WRITING MAKES A PATTERN OF STROKES

Writing an invitation

You could try out the effects of different weights of calligraphy letters by writing an invitation to a party.

1 Make a list of the information your invitation must have on it. (What is happening, where and when.)

Try decorating your invitations with pictures that go with the mood of the party.

2 Decide which words are most important. What do you want to catch the reader's eye first? Which must be biggest?

3 The lettering style can give an impression of what the party will be like. Try out different styles, sizes and weights on scratch paper.

4 When you are happy with the look of the letters, rule up your paper and write out your invitation.

LOOKING AT LAYOUT

The way pictures and writing (text) are arranged on the page is called layout. It is just as important as the lettering style you choose and gives your work its impact. The ideas here will help you decide the best layout for each piece of calligraphy.

Basic layouts

These pictures show five basic ways of laying out your calligraphy. There are many more you can try for yourself.

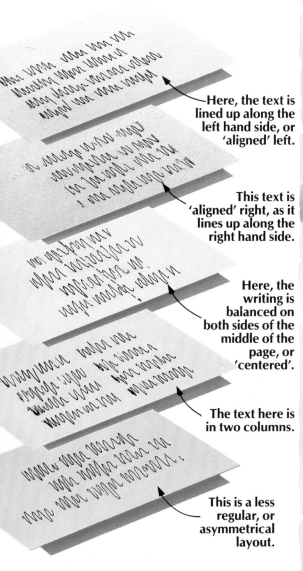

Here, the text is lined up along the left hand side, or 'aligned' left.

This text is 'aligned' right, as it lines up along the right hand side.

Here, the writing is balanced on both sides of the middle of the page, or 'centered'.

The text here is in two columns.

This is a less regular, or asymmetrical layout.

You may find it tricky to choose the best layout for some pieces. Try out as many ideas as you can. In the end, your choice will often be a matter of personal taste.

Unusual layouts

Sometimes you may feel that the overall impact of a piece of calligraphy is more important than being able to read the words easily.

Here are some examples of more unusual layouts. If you want to try some yourself, draw some pencil guidelines of the shape you want before you start writing.

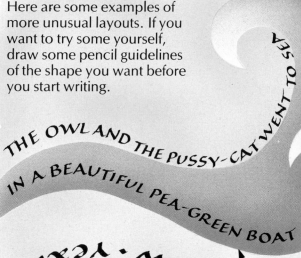

THE OWL AND THE PUSSY-CAT WENT TO SEA
IN A BEAUTIFUL PEA-GREEN BOAT

This layout follows the shape of a wave to create the right mood for this piece.

we. wish. you. a. happy. New. year. christmas. and. a. merry.

These letters have been slightly 'stretched' to fit this layout.

THIS WAY

Start writing in the middle and turn the paper as you write for this layout.

Cut and paste

Here is one way of trying out several possible layouts before writing your final piece. It is called cut and paste.

1 Write your calligraphy piece out very carefully. Use a piece of scratch paper as this is not the finished work.

2 Cut the text into strips of paper, with a line of writing on each strip.

3 Put the strips on top of another sheet of scratch paper. Move them around until you are happy with the way they are arranged.

4 Glue them down with rubber cement. (You can move the strips if you want to with this glue.)

5 Measuring from the top and the sides of the paper, mark where each line begins. Make marks in the same places on your writing paper and rule up.

Choosing margins

The areas of blank page around your calligraphy are called margins. Their size can give your work a spacious, airy feel or a dark, dense look. Here's a simple way of choosing them.

1 It's a good idea to work on a bigger piece of paper than you really need. You can always trim it, but you cannot add anything back on.

2 Cut four long strips of colored cardboard or stiff paper. Stick them together in pairs to make two right angled corners.

3 Lay the two right angles of cardboard around your work. Keep moving them until you are happy with the margin space you can see.

4 Make small pencil marks in each corner to show where you will trim. Remove the cardboard and trim your paper using a ruler and a craft knife or scalpel.

Margin hints

The method of choosing margins above will soon help you judge them by eye. Some pieces can cause problems, however. Here are some tips on solving them.

Extra space at the bottom stops the piece looking as if it is 'falling off' of the paper.

A short, wide piece needs more space at the sides than at the top and the bottom.

Tall, thin work needs less space at the sides and more at the top and bottom.

Gothic Letters

Gothic is one of the most popular calligraphy styles. It is often called Black Letter because of the strong, dark impression the letters make. Gothic makes a dramatic impact on the page, but it is not the best style to use for work that needs to be easy to read as the letters are quite complicated.

Gothic minuscules

All Gothic minuscules are formed from straight strokes, even those that are curved or round in other styles. Ascenders and descenders are short.

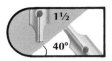

Rule up some paper and copy all the letters, following the numbered strokes and arrows.

Gothic capitals

Gothic capitals are quite tricky to learn. These are a reasonably simple version*. Try writing each letter on tracing paper laid over this page first. When you feel ready, rule up and copy each letter on to paper.

Checkpoint

● Put paper over the top and bottom of some letters. You should see lots of straight strokes, as shown here.

Turn your nib to make this stroke as thin as possible.

*You can find a more complicated Gothic alphabet on page 40.

Writing a certificate

Gothic letters look quite impressive, so they are ideal for official-looking pieces of work.

You could write a certificate using Gothic lettering. It could be a serious award, or a joke, like the one shown here.

1 Decide what words you want on your certificate and what size and weight they should be (see page 13).

2 Write out the words on scratch paper and then choose your layout using cut and paste (see page 15). Rule up a piece of paper ready to write.

3 Load your pen and write the words on your certificate in Gothic letters.

This Certificate is awarded to
JOANNE WATSON
for clearing a path through her room

Signed: *Aremy*
Witness: *FMR*

This is the signature of a 'witness' who agrees the certificate is well-deserved.

A higher quality paper, such as Bristol paper, will make your certificate look more professional.

Making a seal

Old documents often had a wax seal at the bottom. Here's how to make one using two strips of ribbon and a candle.

1 Lay the ribbons on your certificate. Light the candle and let wax drip onto one end of both strips.

2 Wait for the wax to cool slightly. Then press a coin into it. Take the coin off straight up and leave your seal to dry.

Medieval letter

To practice the Gothic style, try writing a 'medieval' letter to a friend. You could use old-fashioned words like 'ye' instead of 'the' and 'thou' instead of 'you'.

Gothic today

Gothic letters are still commonly used today, especially in Germany. People use them for their dramatic effect, as these examples show.

DRACULA

AC/DC

Wurst

17

The Italic Style

Italic is a very popular calligraphy style. It is quicker to write than others and you can adapt it into an elegant handwriting style to use every day, too.

Italic facts

andu   *htlb* — 5° lean

1 The grid that Italic letters are based on is an oval inside a rectangle. The basic shape is an 'a' not an 'o'.

2 The way some Italic letters are written creates small triangles of space between some strokes, like those above.

3 Italic letters lean slightly to the right. Look at the 5° slope of these letters to help you judge how far they should lean.

The Italic alphabet

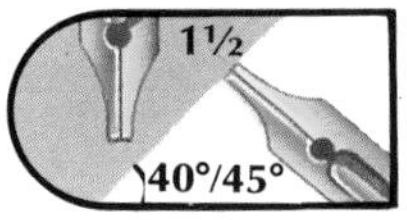

In the Italic alphabet, many pen strokes have built-in 'hook' serifs. These help you start the strokes. Write each letter as smoothly as you can.

a b c d e f g h i j

k l m n o p q r s

'Hook' serif

t u v w x y y z

Italic capitals

Italic capitals are slightly narrower than Roman capitals. They lean about 5° to the right as well. You can find a whole alphabet to copy on page 41.

Added extras

During the Renaissance*, when people first used Italics, they often added decorative strokes to the letters. Some examples are shown below.

If you want to use them, be careful that your work doesn't get too cluttered.

Queen Elizabeth 1 of England used a highly decorative Italic style. She added strokes called flourishes to her signature in 1570.

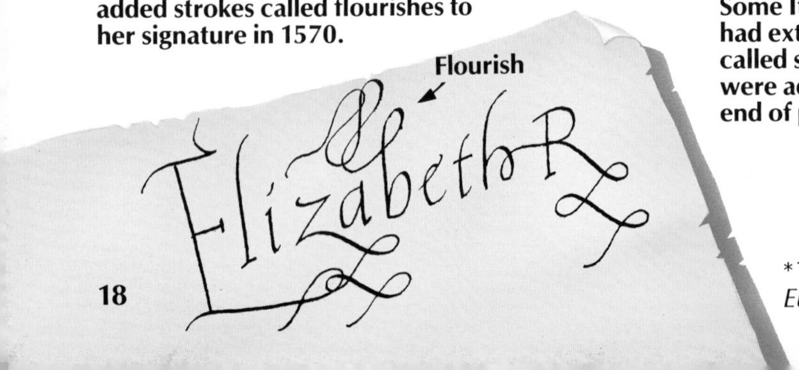

Some writers added loops to their ascenders and descenders.

Loop

h g d f

Some Italic capitals had extra strokes called swashes. They were added to the end of pen strokes.

A N H

Flourish

Elizabeth R

Swash

*This was a time of great artistic activity in Europe, during the 15th and 16th centuries.

Writing a notice

Italics are often used for menus or notices because they are attractive and easy to read. Writing a notice to pin up on a board is a good way to develop a smooth style.

1 Think about what size lettering to use for each piece of information on your notice. Some may be more important than others.

2 Write the words out on scratch paper. Choose the best layout with cut and paste, as shown on page 15.

3 Now write your notice out properly. Try to build up a rhythm of even, sloping pen strokes.

4 When you have finished, pin your work up and stand back to check that the lettering is smooth and clear.

You could cut your notice into an eye-catching shape, like these.

Fly your kite with us

Painting classes Every Monday at the Art Centre 7–9 pm

FOR SALE Fender Stratocaster Excellent condition See Paul Smith

Italic handwriting

For everyday handwriting, try writing Italic letters in one continuous stroke. You will also find it quicker to join some letters together. Here are some of the main ways letters are linked. There is a complete handwriting alphabet on page 42.

1 Extend the 'hook' at the end of a letter up to the top of the next letter.

can

mint

hill ← **'Hook'**

Horizontal stroke

over

wrote

fun

2 Join some letters together with horizontal strokes like those on the left.

3 Some letters, such as 'b', 'p' and 's', look better if only joined together on the left.

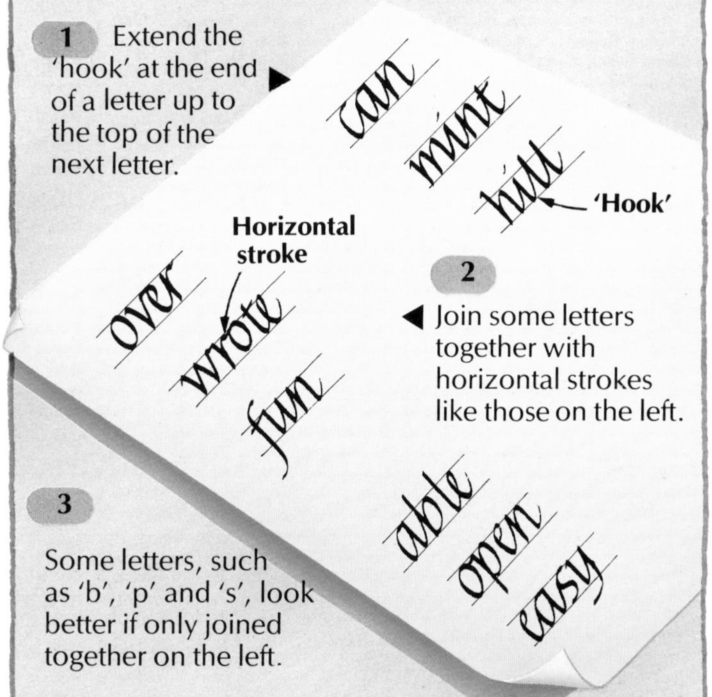

able

open

easy

With practice, you will find you join letters naturally as your own writing style develops.

Using Italic handwriting

Try putting together a folder about a trip or a project. Use your Italic handwriting style for all the writing.

You might find it quicker to write with an Italic fountain pen than with a calligraphy pen. Most art shops sell them.

You could stick your souvenirs at different angles, as shown here, to add interest.

steam train tickets

Our route

TUESDAY The view from the train

The pony near the station

BUILT-UP LETTERS

The letters below are called Versals. They were often used to start a verse or chapter in medieval books. Each part of a Versal is built up with several pen strokes. The outline strokes are made first and then filled in with a central stroke.

Versal facts

   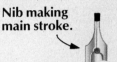

Nib making main stroke.

Nib turned around to make a serif.

In the first picture, the strokes of a Versal 'O' are separated. You write them touching each other to make the finished letter.

Some parts of Versal letters are narrower in the middle. You need to make their two outside strokes curve in slightly, as shown above.

To write the main strokes of Versals, turn your pen to make them as wide as possible. For serifs, turn your nib to make them as thin as you can.

The Versal alphabet

24 nib widths

5

Pen angle: see above

These Versals are not filled in, to show you how they are formed. You can fill them in using the finished Versals on page 41 to check your letters.

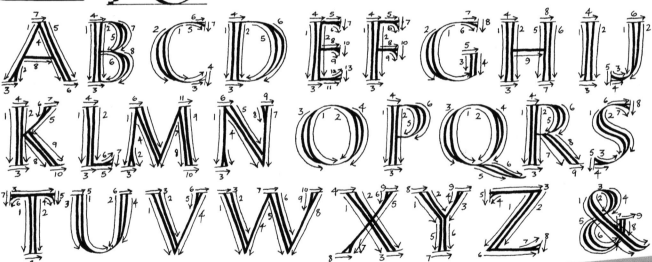

Versatile Versals

Versals are useful for all sorts of pieces. Here are some less traditional ways of using them.

Here, Versals are written at different heights.

These are 'open' Versals, without the center stroke filled in.

20

Painted letters

Large Versals were often painted gold or rich colors in early manuscripts.*

Here's how to fill in the outline of a Versal letter with colored paint. You can adapt this method for other styles of lettering, too.

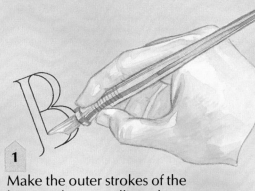

1 Make the outer strokes of the letter with your calligraphy pen, using a thin nib, such as a 5.

2 Once the ink is dry, dip a small brush in watercolor or gouache paint and fill in the letter.

Patterned letters

Write some large letters with wide pens like those on page 5. Trace around their outlines and fill them in with patterns to produce letters like these.

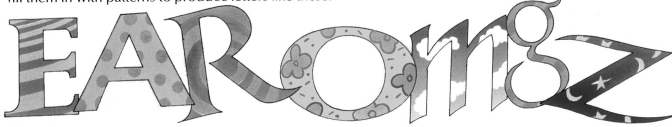

Message on a T-shirt

You can paint letters on materials such as wood or cloth that a pen will not write on. Here's how to paint your own message on a T-shirt.

You will need:

A clean, plain T-shirt (a cotton one is best).

Tracing paper.

A hard and a soft pencil.

A small, pointed paintbrush.

Waterproof fabric paint. (Follow the instructions carefully).

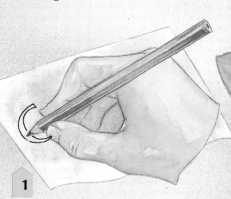

Masking tape

Cardboard

1 Draw the letters onto some tracing-paper with a hard pencil. Turn the sheet over and scribble hard over the back of the letters with a soft pencil.

2 Tape the sheet face up on the T-shirt in the right position. Go over the letters with a hard pencil to transfer them onto the shirt.

3 Put a sheet of cardboard inside the T-shirt. Paint the outline of each letter first and then carefully fill it in with paint using your small paintbrush.

*See page 23 for more about decorating letters.

Decoration and Illumination

Calligraphers throughout history have decorated their work. Your decoration can be quite simple and still look effective, as these ideas show.

Beautiful borders

A patterned border makes an attractive frame for calligraphy.

There are more border patterns on page 45.

Load some ink into your calligraphy pen and make a pattern of pen strokes around the edge of your writing paper.

Don't make it too wide, or it will overpower your lettering.

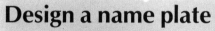

Try writing the alphabet you are using, your name, or the title of the piece in a border around your work.

Here are some ideas to try.

Move the stencil around the edges.

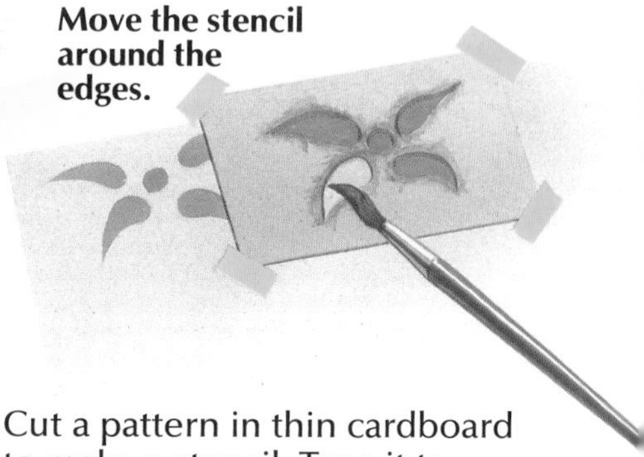

Cut a pattern in thin cardboard to make a stencil. Tape it to each edge of your work. Add color through the holes*.

Pen pictures

You can draw pictures with your pen to decorate your calligraphy.

1 Draw or trace a picture or cartoon onto your paper with a fairly hard pencil.

2 Draw over the pencil lines with your calligraphy pen, using a medium or narrow nib.

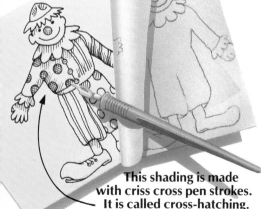

This shading is made with criss cross pen strokes. It is called cross-hatching.

Design a name plate

You could combine lettering and decoration by designing a name plate on thin cardboard for your bedroom door.

The designs shown here will give you some ideas for choosing decoration that matches your lettering style.

A border of straight pen strokes goes well with dark Gothic letters.

Richard

Delicate drawings look best with Italics.

Lucy

JOHN

These Roman capitals go well with geometric shapes.

*You can find out more about stencils on page 34.

Illumination

In the Middle Ages, capital letters were often richly decorated, like the one on the left. Adding the gold and then color decoration was called illuminating the letter. You can find out how to do it below.

This illuminated capital is based on a traditional design.

The text was arranged around an illuminated capital as shown here.

Cheap gold

Here are some more cheap materials which will also color your work gold.

This gold gouache paint can be used on its own or mixed with water.

Gold felt-tip pens are good for outlines but the ink can develop a dark outline, or 'halo' on the page.

This gold-colored powder can be mixed with gum arabic (from art shops) and water, then loaded into a pen.

Gilding

In illumination, the gold is applied before any color. This is called gilding.

Real gold leaf is very expensive. The method shown here uses thin sheets of gold called transfer gold which is inexpensive. Good art shops sell it.

You will need:

Glue

A tube of gouache paint* (any color).

Mix the same amount of glue and water and add a little gouache

A sheet of transfer gold.

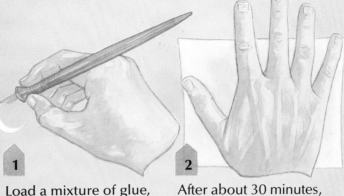

1 Load a mixture of glue, water and a little gouache into your pen. Write the letter outline, then carefully fill it in.

2 After about 30 minutes, breathe on the letter to make it sticky again. Put the transfer gold over it and press down firmly.

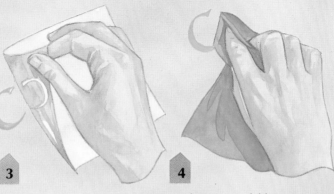

3 Take the sheet off. If gold has not stuck to the whole letter, repeat step 2 until it is covered.

4 Rub your gold letter carefully with a soft piece of cloth to make it shine. This is called burnishing.

Decoration

Add decoration around your gilded letter that suits the purpose of the piece. Here are some examples.

You could add sparkles to a letter.

Try decorating your letter with flowers.

Illuminate a letter with simple pictures.

You can find out more about gouache paint on page 32.

Cards and Presents

You can use your calligraphy skills to make original cards and presents.

Paper and cardboard

You can make cards out of many different sorts of paper or cardboard. Below are the main types of paper and cardboard available, with tips on when to use them.

Layout paper is ideal for scratch paper and for some finished work.

Bristol paper gives a 'classier' look to cards, certificates and posters.

Ingres and Caslon papers are easy to write on and look good.

Handmade paper is expensive, but is ideal for special pieces of work.

Textured paper produces interesting lettering effects.

Art shops stock thin cardboard in many thicknesses and colors.

Making cards

There are lots of different ways to fold a card. Each one has a different effect. Try folding a sheet of scratch paper in some of the ways shown below to give you some ideas for making your own cards.

HAPPY BIRTHDAY

Merry Christmas

BONNE CHANCE PAUL

GLÜCK WUNSCHE!

Félicitations

This card was folded in half diagonally and then in half again.

NOËL

A concertina card

Here's a card which is ideal for writing a joke or a rhyme inside.

You will need:
A sheet of cardboard about 4 inches x 1 foot.
16 inches of ribbon.
A hole punch.

2 inches

If your card has six sections, each one is 2 inches wide.

Middle of fold

1 Figure out the number of lines in your joke or rhyme. Fold the card backwards and forwards into equal sections like a concertina.

2 Rule up and write one line on each section, starting at the top.

3 Mark the middle of each alternate fold, starting at the top. Punch a hole through each mark.

4 With the card still folded, thread the ribbon through the holes and tie the ends in a bow.

Writing on glass

You can even paint some calligraphy on a glass. Here's how to do it.

To figure out how big your letters should be, write them in several sizes on some paper and hold them against the glass.

1

Tape the paper 'pattern' you choose to the inside of the glass where you want the letters to be.

2

Ease the paper up against the curved part of the glass.

Using a small paintbrush and waterproof paint, such as enamel, carefully paint in the letters.

3

Wipe mistakes off while the paint is still wet, using a rag dipped in turpentine or white spirit*.

When the paint is dry, take the pattern out. Wash the glass out thoroughly with hot soapy water.

4

You can find out how to make calligraphy wrapping paper and gift tags on pages 34 and 35.

Framing your calligraphy

Framed calligraphy looks more professional. Here's how to make a simple frame.

Leave 1 inch extra paper outside your margins (see page 15). Cut two pieces of cardboard or mounting board* to the same size as your worksheet.

1

1 inch extra

Put spots of glue around the edge of a sheet of cardboard. Lay your worksheet on the cardboard, put some tracing paper over it and press down with your palm.

2

Measure and mark a 1 inch strip around the second sheet of cardboard. Put your ruler against each line and cut the center out, leaving a frame.

3

Don't cut right to the edge.

Put spots of glue around the edge of one side of the frame. Place it carefully over your worksheet so that the edges line up. Press down firmly.

4

Edges aligned

Tape a loop of ribbon or a curtain ring onto the back sheet of cardboard if you want to hang your frame on the wall.

5

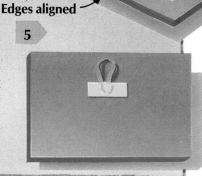

---

*You can buy these liquids from hardware shops. Take great care as they are poisonous.

*Mounting board is available from art shops.

CHINESE CALLIGRAPHY

Chinese calligraphy looks uncluttered and spacious. It is traditionally written with a bamboo brush. You can use one to give your calligraphy an Oriental look, too.

Chinese brushes

Here are some of the brushes Chinese calligraphers use. You can get them at good art shops. A wide bamboo brush with bristles is the best one to start with.

Preparing to write

You need to lay your drawing board flat for Oriental calligraphy. The different strokes are made by varying how hard you press your brush down.

1 Tape some scratch paper (newspaper is ideal) under your writing sheet. This will soak up moisture from your brush strokes.

2 Dip the whole brush in water and then the last ⅔ of the bristles at the tip, in ink.

3 Hold the brush upright, with your fingers arranged as shown in the picture below.

4 Try making the strokes shown on the right. How to do each one is explained next to it.

A peacock feather brush

A soft duck-down brush

Bamboo brushes with bristle tips

Start with light pressure on the tip, press down harder, then lift the brush up slowly for this stroke.

Flick the brush tip away from you to make these strokes.

Lay the whole brush down and then lift it up to get these short strokes.

Lay the brush down and twist it to make small circles.

Drag the brush up the page, lifting it gradually as you write.

Lay the bristles down flat on the paper. Push the brush away from you.

Ink stones

Chinese calligraphers use ink made by grinding an ink stick with a little water in an ink stone. Some art shops sell them if you want to try it.

Ink stick   Ink stone

Writing a Chinese character

The Chinese alphabet is made up of characters. A character stands for an idea, not just one letter. Each character has several types of brush strokes.

There is not enough room to show the whole alphabet here, but this character contains the eight basic strokes of Chinese calligraphy. They are all made by varying the pressure you put on the brush, as shown on page 26.

Following the direction of the arrows with your brush, make each stroke of the character in the right order. Don't worry if you need to practice this several times before it looks right.

This character means 'eternity' in Chinese.

Making a Chinese scroll

Chinese characters are usually written one under the other, not across the page. The three characters below mean 'long life, good luck and happiness'. Try writing them on a long sheet of paper to look like an Oriental scroll.

To write the characters, follow the arrows below, in order, with your brush.

These pictures were made up of some of the brush strokes on the opposite page.

Brush pictures

You can easily give other calligraphy styles a spacious, Oriental 'feel'. You could write the words one under the other, or add brush stroke illustrations like the ones shown here.

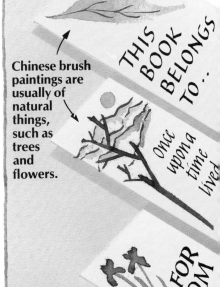

Chinese brush paintings are usually of natural things, such as trees and flowers.

THIS BOOK BELONGS TO...

Once upon a time lived

FOR MOM

DIFFERENT TOOLS

You don't always have to use a calligraphy pen to write calligraphy letters, as you saw on pages 26-27.

It is a good idea to try out as many different writing tools as you can, or even make your own as shown on pages 4-5.

Calligraphy brushes

Art shops sell broad-edged calligraphy brushes like the ones below. They are not expensive and come in several sizes. Here you can see some of the effects they create. There is a complete brush alphabet to try on page 43.

Wide brushes make very large, heavyweight strokes like these.

A medium brush was dipped in watered-down ink to create this effect.

A small brush was dipped in ink and then wiped with a tissue to make these strokes.

Automatic pens

The two pens below are called automatic pens. They have wide, split nibs and are useful for creating special effects or writing wide strokes. You can buy them from art shops.

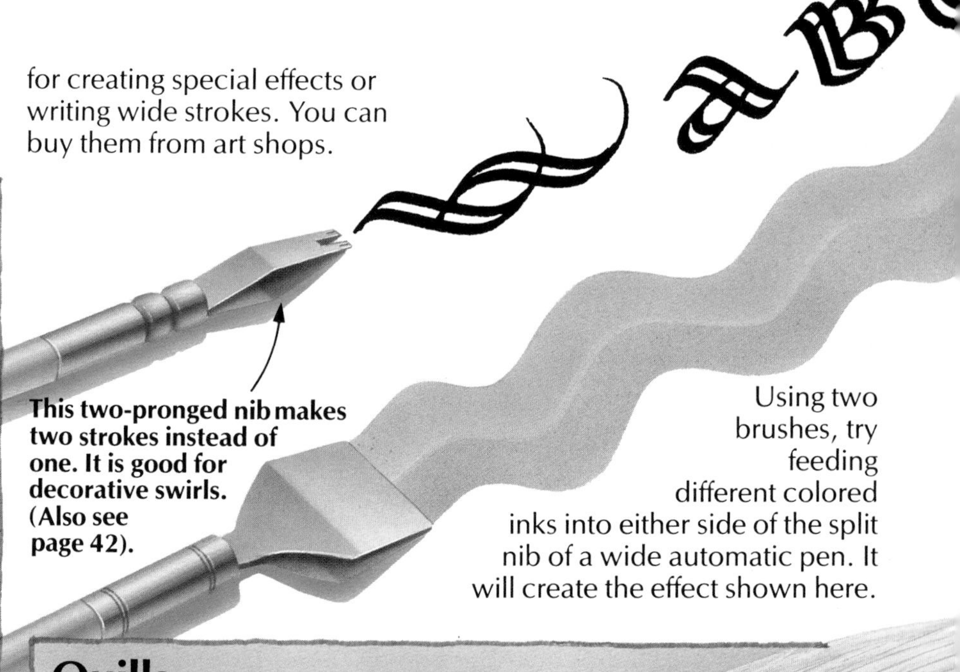

Loading automatic pens

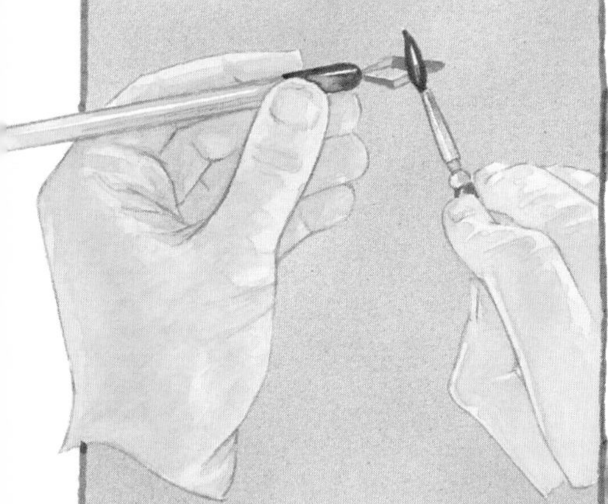

This two-pronged nib makes two strokes instead of one. It is good for decorative swirls. (Also see page 42).

Using two brushes, try feeding different colored inks into either side of the split nib of a wide automatic pen. It will create the effect shown here.

To load your pen, dip a brush in ink and wipe it against the inside bottom edge of the nib on both sides. Ink will collect behind the writing-edge.

Quills

Quills are pens made from birds' feathers. Cutting a quill yourself is very tricky. There are books that give precise instructions if you want to try it (see page 47).

Some art shops sell ready-cut quills, like this one.

28

Making your own pens

Here are two simple writing tools you can make yourself. You need to use a sharp craft knife, so be careful not to cut yourself. Always cut away from yourself.†

Bamboo pens

Bamboo canes were first made into pens thousands of years ago. You can make one with a piece of medium-width garden cane about 4 inches long.

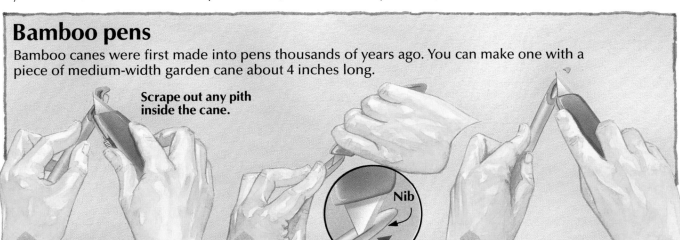

Scrape out any pith inside the cane.

Nib

1 Lay the cane flat on your drawing board. Hold your knife slanting away from you and slice 1 inch off the tip.

2 Rest the end of the cane on the edge of your drawing board. Cut a slit about ½ inch long down the middle of it.†

3 Trim off the last ¹⁄₁₀ inch of the nib. Load your cane with plenty of ink with a brush and it is ready to write with.

Balsa pens

A sheet of balsa wood 4 inches wide and ⅕ inch thick will make several calligraphy 'pens'. You can buy it from most craft shops quite inexpensively.

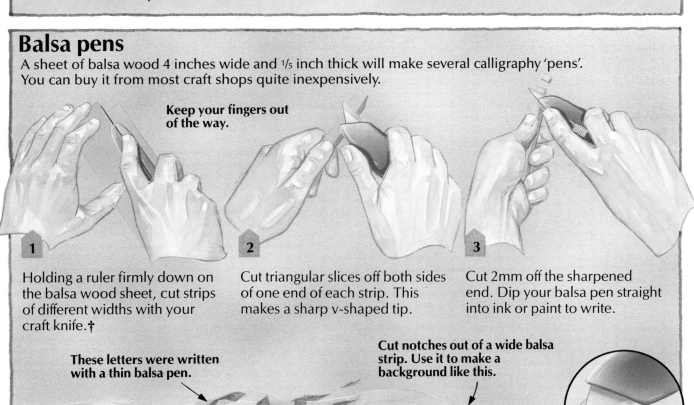

Keep your fingers out of the way.

1 Holding a ruler firmly down on the balsa wood sheet, cut strips of different widths with your craft knife.†

2 Cut triangular slices off both sides of one end of each strip. This makes a sharp v-shaped tip.

3 Cut 2mm off the sharpened end. Dip your balsa pen straight into ink or paint to write.

These letters were written with a thin balsa pen.

Cut notches out of a wide balsa strip. Use it to make a background like this.

CAFÉ

DESIGNING AN ALPHABET

You don't just have to use the lettering styles in this book. Here you can find out how to adapt them, or design a completely new alphabet yourself.

Changing letters

You can use some of the techniques you have learned in this book to change the look of a lettering style.

Here are three ways you can adapt letters.

1

You can use different nibs and x-heights to change the letter's weight (see pages 12-13).

These Foundational letters were written with a narrow nib.

pqrs

2

Try writing with a different tool, such as a brush instead of a pen.

These Uncials were written with a medium calligraphy brush.

pqr

3

You can exaggerate some features of the letters, or add extra strokes.

These Italic letters have extra strokes called swashes.

PQR

Your own alphabet

Here are the steps used to create the alphabet at the bottom of the page. You can follow them to invent an alphabet of your own.

1 Fit a wide nib, such as a 1 ½, into your calligraphy pen. You can try out other nibs later if you want to.

2 Choose the look you want your alphabet to have. Then think about what features will achieve it.

fsgmh

Try out lots of different looks.

o

This 'O' is the basic shape for the alphabet below.

8o

3 Decide on the shape of your 'O' first. This will affect the shape of every other letter in your alphabet.

4 Write your alphabet out in the groups of letters below. You will need to vary the pen angle for the diagonal group to make the letters of your alphabet look consistent.

Narrow letters

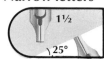

LLEFJ K B
PR5

Round letters

O Q D C G

Rectangular letters

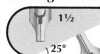

H T V Z

Hold your nib at less of an angle to make this stroke.

Diagonal letters

A M N V W
X Y

Personal stationery

You could use your alphabet to personalize some stationery with your name and address. If you use black ink, you can take photocopies of the original sheet.

1
Write out your name and address several times in your alphabet. The letters can be any size you like.

2
Use the cut and paste method on page 15 to try out different layouts on top of a sheet of writing paper.

3
When you have chosen a layout, rule some lines the right distance apart and write the calligraphy.

Logos

You could make an attractive design, or logo, out of your initials written in your alphabet. You can use it on your stationery.

Rubber stamps

You can cut letters into an eraser to make a stamp. Try designing a logo of a friend's initials and cutting it into an eraser. Give it with an ink stamp pad from an art shop as a present.

You will need:
Tracing paper
Ink stamp pad
Medium-sized firm eraser
Pencil
Scalpel

The letters print the right way

1
Write the logo on tracing paper with a soft pencil. Turn the sheet over. Use a hard pencil to trace it backwards onto the eraser.

2
Cut around the outline of the letters with a scalpel. Angle the blade outwards from the letter strokes slightly.†

3
Gradually slice off the eraser around the letters until they are left standing about 2mm above the surface.

4
Press the raised letters onto the ink stamp, and then onto paper. If the are not clear, trim any rough edges.

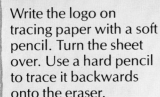

31

Calligraphy and Color

There are lots of ways you can make your calligraphy colorful. Some ideas for colored letters and backgrounds are shown here.

Writing with gouache

You can use gouache paint for writing calligraphy. Art shops sell a selection of colors in tubes or jars.

1 Put a little gouache into a small jar. Add a little water and mix until it is a creamy consistency.

2 Leave the mixture to stand for a few hours. Load it into your calligraphy pen with a brush.

Color choices

It's worth spending time choosing colors and trying different combinations.

The colors you choose combine with the lettering style to create the 'look' of each piece of work.

These 'warm' colors create a passionate, fiery, or exciting feeling.

These 'cool' colors help create a calm, peaceful feeling.

These two very different colors make a striking impact.

Pale letters on a dark background and dark letters on a paler background look dramatic.

Colors that are only slightly different give this soft effect.

Changing colors

Try loading your pen with a slightly different color gouache after writing a few letters. Don't wash it out between colors. Mix your paints in a ice cube tray, starting at the top row, then going back to the second.

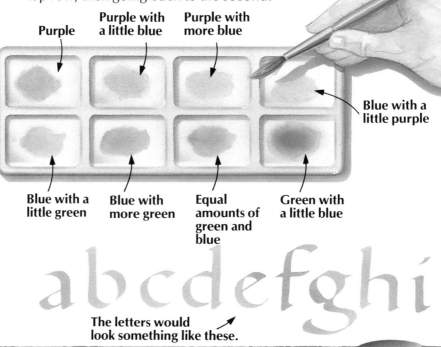

Purple

Purple with a little blue

Purple with more blue

Blue with a little purple

Blue with a little green

Blue with more green

Equal amounts of green and blue

Green with a little blue

The letters would look something like these.

Colored inks

You can use colored waterproof inks straight from the jar, but they can produce patchy lettering and may clog your pen.

A color wash

You could try brushing watered down gouache or watercolor paint over white paper to make a subtly colored background. This is called a color wash.

1 Float the paper in water for about a minute. Tape it flat on your drawing board with brown gummed tape from an art shop. Let the paper dry.

2 Brush the paper with water and then with watered-down paint. The more watery the paint mixture, the paler the background will be.

3 When the paper is dry, write the calligraphy. Choose a strong color so that the letters stand out clearly.

Washing over wax

You can add a color wash over calligraphy letters if you write them with a rubbed-down wax crayon, as shown on page 5. The example below was written with a white crayon.

1 Using your rubbed-down crayon, write some calligraphy letters on a sheet of white paper.

2 Follow the steps on the left to give the sheet a color wash.

Invisible letters

You can create interesting letter effects by using masking fluid from an art shop. Its fumes are poisonous, so only use it in an airy room. Wash your nib out afterwards.

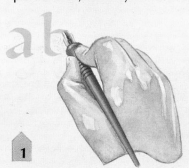

1 Pour some masking fluid into a saucer. Load your pen with fluid, using a brush, and write some letters.

2 Dip an old toothbrush in paint, hold it over the letters and gently pull a matchstick along the top of the bristles.

3 Rub the letters with your fingertip. They will 'appear' in the spattered paint where the fluid 'masked' the paper.

STENCILS AND RUBBINGS

Letter shapes can be cut out as well as written. Here you can find out how to use cut-out calligraphy letters to make stencils and letter rubbings.

Making stencils

You can make a stencil using any of the lettering styles in this book. It is best to use waxed stencil paper from an art shop, but thin cardboard will do.

1
Write some large letters on layout paper. Then, go around the outline of each one with a pencil on tracing paper.

2
Trace the letters onto your stencil paper or cardboard. Make thin strokes thicker as it will be easier to cut them out.

Middle piece from letter 'a'.

3
Carefully cut around the letters with a craft knife or scalpel to make a stencil. Keep the 'middles' that fall out. †

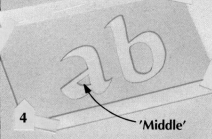

'Middle'

4
Tape your stencil to a piece of layout paper with masking tape. Stick any 'middles' in place with glue or rubber cement.

5 Be careful not to move the 'middle'.
Color through the 'gaps' in your stencil with pencil, crayons or a cotton swab dipped in paint.

6
Carefully take the stencil and middles off the paper. Keep them so you can build up a 'library' of stencils.

Stylish stencils

Some ways you could use stencils are shown here. For a more ambitious project, try stenciling a border of calligraphy letters around your room.

Stencil a whole phrase as many times as you like onto a sheet of paper to make original wrapping paper.

Here, stencils were taped to a mug and a plate and painted with waterproof enamel paint.

Letter rubbings

Try putting paper over your calligraphy stencils or cut-out letters. Then rub across them with a soft pencil or wax crayon. This is called taking a rubbing.

Rub all around the letter, as shown here.

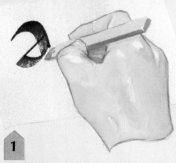

1

Cut the letters you want out of thin cardboard, as on the page opposite. This time, you will use the pieces you cut out.

2

Stick the letters onto a piece of cardboard with rubber cement in any layout you choose. This makes your rubbing board.

3

Put a piece of layout paper over the rubbing board. Gently rub a crayon or soft pencil over the whole sheet to make a rubbing.

Making gift tags

You could make gift tags with letter rubbings on them. Punch a hole and thread a ribbon through each one to tie it to a gift.

Use thin cardboard as it is stronger than paper and should still make clear rubbings.

Cut your tags into different shapes after you have rubbed over them.

Choose a color crayon that will show up clearly on top of the colored cardboard.

Colorful collage

Try doing a large poster made up of a collage of calligraphy letter rubbings.

This letter was cut from corrugated cardboard to make a textured rubbing.

EMBOSSING AND INCISING

Two more advanced techniques you can use with calligraphy letters are shown here. They are called embossing and incising.

Embossing

Embossed letters are not written, but 'molded' in paper, Here's a basic embossing technique to try using simple, inexpensive equipment.

You will need:
A thin sheet of cardboard.
A round-ended paintbrush.
A sheet of layout paper.
A craft knife or scalpel.
A sheet of medium-thickness Bristol paper.
A soft and a hard pencil.

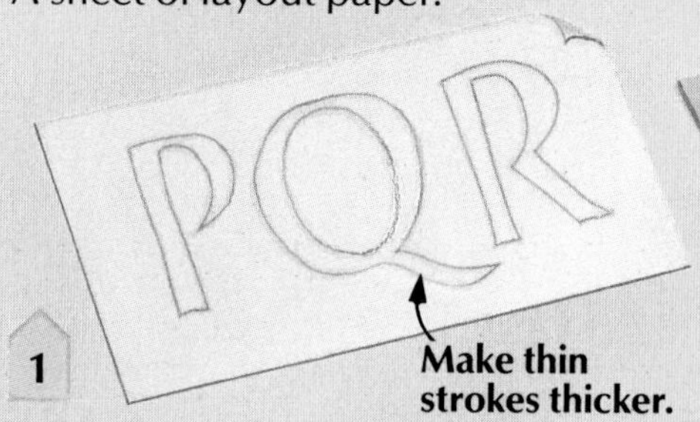

1

Make thin strokes thicker.

Draw the outline of some large letters on a sheet of layout paper with a soft pencil.

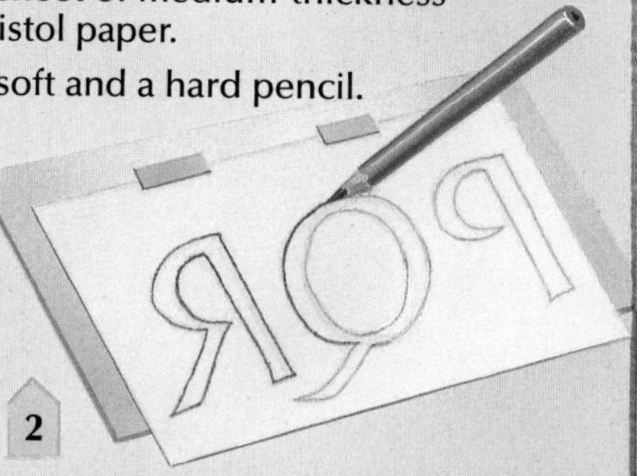

2

Turn the paper over. Tape it onto the thin cardboard. Go over the backward letters with a hard pencil.

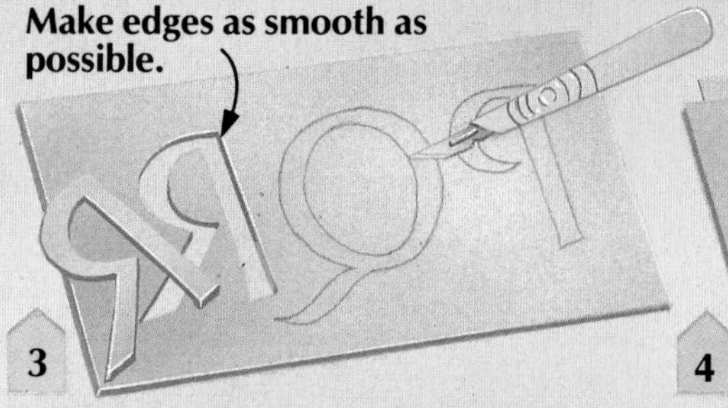

3

Make edges as smooth as possible.

The letters will be backwards on the cardboard. Cut them out with a sharp craft knife or scalpel.†

4

Glue the cardboard on top of a second sheet of cardboard. Then lay the thick paper over them.

5

Don't rub too hard or the paper might tear.

Gently rub the paper into the letter 'molds' with the rounded end of your paintbrush.

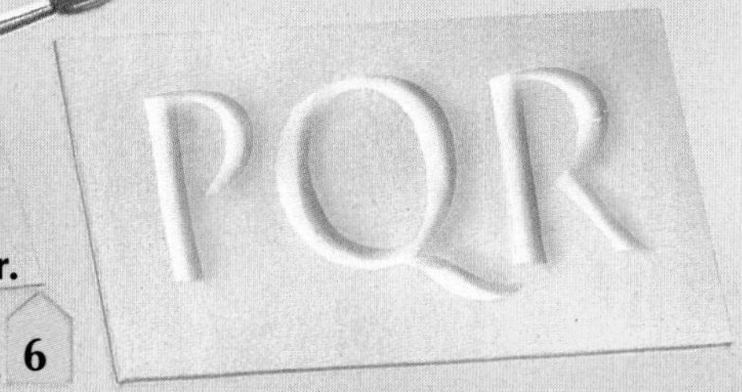

6

Turn the paper over. Your embossed letters should be raised above the surface of the paper.

Embossing effects

Embossed letters look very sophisticated. Here are some ways you could use them.

Invitations are often embossed.

Embossed writing paper is very stylish.

This stands for 'répondez s'il vous plaît', or 'please reply', in French.

Make an embossed paper cover to go around a book.

Light and shade

Embossed letters cast soft shadows. Hang some embossing on a wall and try lighting it from different angles to get the best effect.

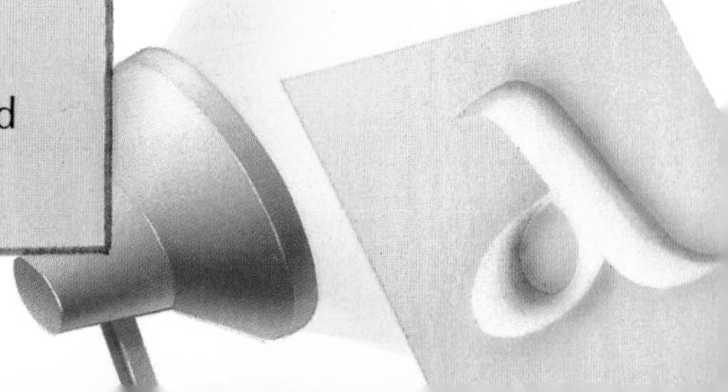

Incising

Incised letters are carved into something solid, such as stone or clay. You can incise most calligraphy styles, but Roman capitals are good to start with as they produce the best effects.

You will need:
A sheet of thin cardboard

A scalpel

A rolling pin or bottle

Modeling clay

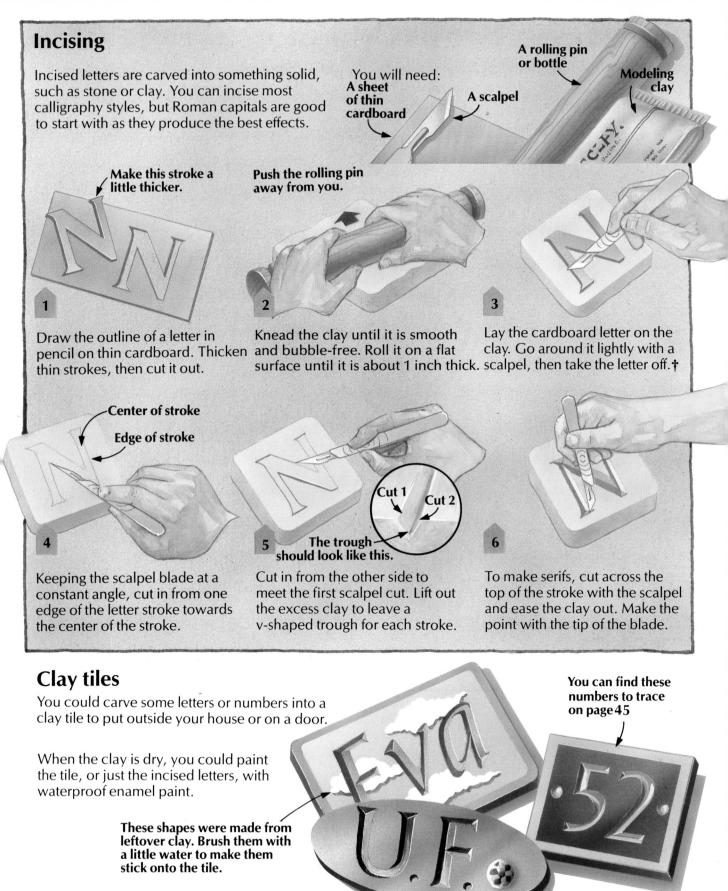

Make this stroke a little thicker.

1

Draw the outline of a letter in pencil on thin cardboard. Thicken thin strokes, then cut it out.

Push the rolling pin away from you.

2

Knead the clay until it is smooth and bubble-free. Roll it on a flat surface until it is about 1 inch thick.

3

Lay the cardboard letter on the clay. Go around it lightly with a scalpel, then take the letter off.†

Center of stroke

Edge of stroke

4

Keeping the scalpel blade at a constant angle, cut in from one edge of the letter stroke towards the center of the stroke.

5

Cut 1   **Cut 2**

The trough should look like this.

Cut in from the other side to meet the first scalpel cut. Lift out the excess clay to leave a v-shaped trough for each stroke.

6

To make serifs, cut across the top of the stroke with the scalpel and ease the clay out. Make the point with the tip of the blade.

Clay tiles

You could carve some letters or numbers into a clay tile to put outside your house or on a door.

You can find these numbers to trace on page 45

When the clay is dry, you could paint the tile, or just the incised letters, with waterproof enamel paint.

These shapes were made from leftover clay. Brush them with a little water to make them stick onto the tile.

Careers and Calligraphy

Becoming a professional calligrapher is not easy. You will need to do some further training. Most calligraphers don't work full-time for one company but take on projects from different companies.

Further study

You can study calligraphy on full-time or part-time courses. Write to the addresses on page 47 for details.

Full-time courses

●You can study calligraphy as one option on some Graphic Design courses. Entry requirements vary, but it would be useful to study Art or Technical Drawing.

●There are a few specialist calligraphy courses. You don't need specific qualifications to take one, but must show promise as a calligrapher.

Part-time courses

●Many areas run calligraphy evening classes, summer schools or correspondence courses.

Preparing your portfolio

Select pieces of your work that show off your calligraphy skills best. They make up what is called your portfolio.

You can buy a flat case to keep your work in, also called a portfolio. On page 47 you can find out how to make a simpler one yourself.

Portfolio

MERRY CHRISTMAS

The leaves fluttered in the wind restlessly

Getting work

Your first job is always the hardest to find. After that, customers may use you again or recommend you to others. Here are some ways to look for work.

●Make a list of possible clients in your area, such as schools, small businesses or card shops.

●Call their receptionist to find out the best person for you to contact at each one.

●Write to them, saying you are starting out as a calligrapher. Offer to visit them to show them your portfolio.

Companies need headed stationery.

Certificate of merit awarded to Elizabeth Smith

·ALPHA·GRAPHICS·

TAXI 0·372·4160

Schools often award certificates that are written in calligraphy.

Business card

● When they see your portfolio, draw their attention to pieces that are especially relevant to their needs.

●If they ask you to do some work for them, you can find out how to go about it on the page opposite.

A professional job

Below are the steps a professional calligrapher takes to design a calendar for a local company.

1 The client tells the calligrapher exactly what the job involves. These details form what is called a brief for the job.

2 If both are happy to go ahead, the client asks, or commissions him to do it. They agree on a delivery date and a fee.

Thumbnails

3 In the studio, the calligrapher makes small sketches of possible layouts for the piece. These are called 'thumbnails'.

4 The calligrapher tries out several styles, weights and sizes of calligraphy letters. Cut and paste helps him find the best layout.

5 The calligrapher discusses his ideas and thumbnails with the client. They select the layout they feel fulfils the brief best.

6 The calligrapher assembles the equipment for the job. In a quiet room to help concentration, he writes the finished piece.

7 The work is delivered to the client. If it is on time and is satisfactory, the calligrapher is paid the agreed fee.

Other careers

The lettering skills you learn while doing calligraphy can be useful in other careers too.

Signwriting

Many signs outside shops and restaurants are hand-painted by professional signwriters. The equipment is slightly different from a calligrapher's, but the skills are very similar.

This hand-painted sign is for a French restaurant.

Careers using type

Many styles of type, or typefaces, are influenced by calligraphy styles. Skill in choosing the right one could be useful if you want to work in publishing, journalism or advertising.

Menu

This typeface is closely based on the Gothic calligraphy style. It helps give this menu a traditional, old-fashioned feel.

This typeface gives this shampoo an elegant, feminine appeal. It is called an Italic typeface. The letters lean to the right, like calligraphy Italics.

Lustre

This plain, sans serif type could be used in children's books as it is easy to read.

Story

Alphabets to copy · 1

On the next five pages, you will find ten more alphabets to try. There are suggestions on where to use them in your calligraphy, too.

Roman capitals

The Roman capitals made by following the skeleton letters on page 8 should look like the letters below. They go well with most styles of minuscules. You can add serifs or leave them sans serif (see page 9). These letters are sans serif.

ABCDEFGHIJ
KLMNOPQRS
TUVWXYZ

Ornate Gothic

These Gothic capitals are more ornate than those on page 16. They will also take longer to write as they have more strokes. Use them with the minuscules also on page 16.

Italic capitals

Italic capitals are most commonly used with Italic minuscules as they both lean 5° to the right (see page 18). They can be effective when combined with other styles, too.

ABCDEFGHIJKLMN
OPQRSTUVWXYZ

Swash capitals

These letters are called Swash Italic capitals, as they have added strokes called swashes (see page 18). Keep them short or they will clash with other lines of text.

ABCDEFG

Filled Versals

The Versal strokes shown on page 20 should make letters like those below. They go well with most minuscule styles. Try writing them with a wide brush for posters.

ABCDEFGHI

JKLMNOPQR

STUVWXYZ

Alphabets to copy · 2

The six minuscule alphabets on this page have very different 'looks'. They are written with a variety of calligraphy tools. Each one creates a different effect.

Carolingian minuscules

The letters below are called Carolingian minuscules. They were the first real small letters (see page 2). They look best when used with large Uncials or Versals.

Split nib alphabet

The letters below were written with an automatic pen with a split nib, called a scroll pen. They are based on Italics, so follow the strokes as shown on page 18.

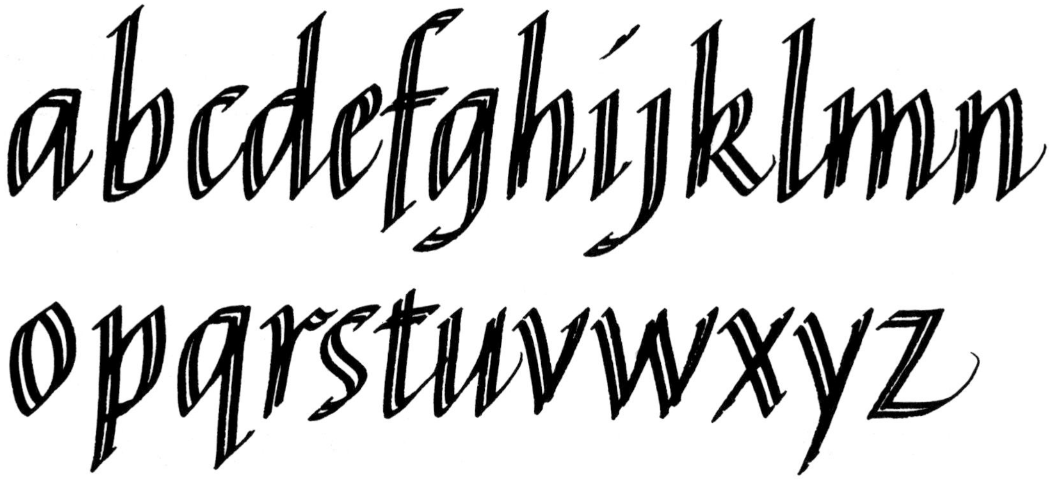

abcdefghijklmn

opqrstuvwxyz

Handwriting alphabet

This is an Italic handwriting alphabet. It shows how each letter should be joined to other letters. Try writing the alphabet joined together as shown here to increase your speed and develop a smooth style.

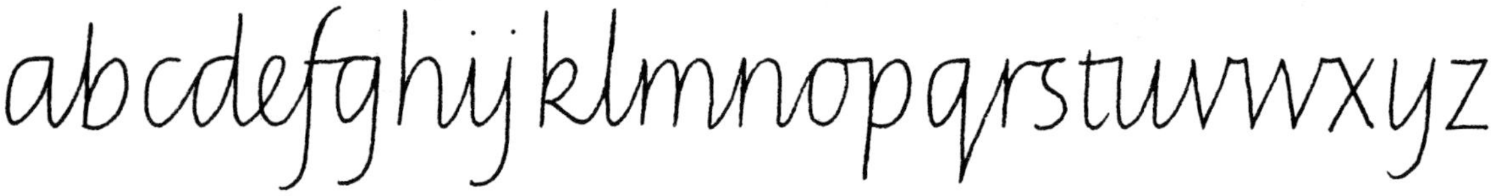

abcdefghijklmnopqrstuvwxyz

Brush alphabet

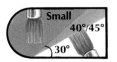

These Foundational letters (see page 11), were written with a small calligraphy brush dipped in watered-down ink.

Two original alphabets

The two alphabets below were designed by a calligrapher called Solos Solou. They both have an 'Eastern' feel.

This alphabet was written with a narrow automatic pen. Twist the nib to form a steeper angle (45°) to make the vertical strokes get thinner at the bottom.

Ascenders are twice as high as the body of each letter.

43

Alphabets to copy·3

You could trace off the outlines of the two alphabets on this page and use them for illumination, embossing, posters or stenciling.

Outline alphabet

The thin strokes of these outline letters have been made slightly thicker. This makes them easier to trace around and cut out.

Type alphabet

This is a style of type, or typeface, called Optima. Here it is printed very big and bold (heavyweight) to make it easier to trace around.

It was designed by a calligrapher called Hermann Zapf. Optima letters have thick and thin strokes, like calligraphy letters.

If you look closely, you will see that all the type in this book is Optima, used in different sizes and weights.

Thick stroke

Thin stroke

a b c d e f g h i
j k l m n o p q
r s t u v w x y z

Numbers and patterns

Here are some numbers and more border patterns, to use in your calligraphy.

Chinese numbers

Write these Chinese numbers with a bamboo brush (see page 26).

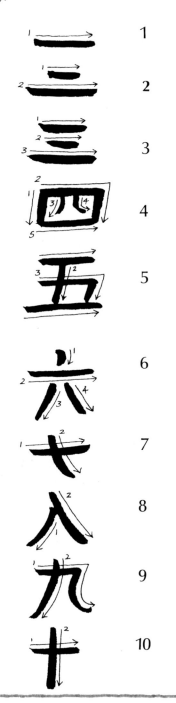

1
2
3
4
5
6
7
8
9
10

Arabic numbers

The numbers used in most Western countries are called Arabic numbers. You can use them with all the calligraphy styles in this book. Make them the same size and weight as the letters in the piece.

Continental seven

Italic numbers

For Italic calligraphy, make the numbers slightly narrower, like the ones shown here. They should also lean 5° to the right.

0 1 2 3 4 5 6 7 7 8 9

Punctuation

You can use these punctuation marks with all the calligraphy styles in this book.

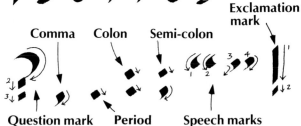

Comma   Colon   Semi-colon   Exclamation mark

Question mark   Period   Speech marks

Patterned borders

Here are some more borders, made with a calligraphy pen. Choose one which goes well with your lettering style (see page 22 for some hints).

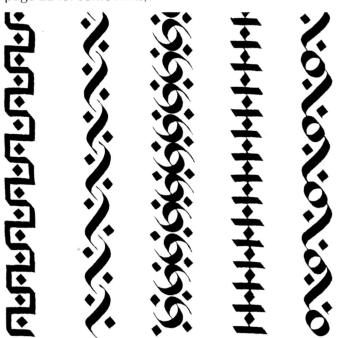

45

Glossary

aligned left: each line of text starts at the same point on the left-hand **margin**.

aligned right: each line ends at the same point on the right-hand **margin**. They start at different points on the left.

arched letter: letter which has an arch that springs away from the central **stroke** or **stem**.

ascender: **stroke** going up from the main **body** of a **lower-case letter**, or **minuscule**.

asymmetrical layout: lines of text placed irregularly on the page.

base line: line on which capital letters are written and the **body** of a **minuscule** rests. Also called the **writing line**.

basic shape: the letter which influences the shape of all other letters in a calligraphy style. Usually an 'o'.

body: main part of a **minuscule**, which forms the letter's **x-height**.

brief: details of a piece of work, given to an artist by a client.

built-up letter: a letter in which each part is made up of several **strokes**.

burnish: to make something shine, such as the **gilding**.

capital letter: large or **upper-case letter**. Also called a **majuscule**.

centered layout: lines of **text** balanced on both sides of the middle of the page.

character: a single letter. In Chinese script, each character represents a whole idea.

commission: to ask a calligrapher to do some work for an agreed fee.

condense: to make letters smaller, more narrow or rearrange them so that they take up less space.

crossbar: stroke across the upper part of the letters 't' and 'f' and the middle of 'A' and 'H'.

cross-hatching: shading with parallel or criss-crossed lines.

cursive writing: writing in which some letters are joined together for speed. Usually handwriting.

cut and paste: technique of cutting paper with **text** on it into strips and sticking them down in different **layouts** to judge their effect.

descender: **stroke** going down from the main **body** of a **lower-case letter** (**minuscule**).

diagonal letter: letter which has **strokes** which go in a diagonal direction, such as 'z','v','w' and 'x'.

emboss: to shape paper in some areas by pressing it into or over a mold.

flourish: extra, decorative **stroke**.

gilding: covering a surface with a thin layer of gold, or gold color.

grain (paper): the direction in which most fibers lie in a sheet of paper.

grid: framework of lines and curves on which letters are based.

guidelines: pencil lines between which calligraphy is written to make sure it is straight.

illumination: decoration of a piece of calligraphy with gold and color.

incise: to carve letters in a hard substance such as stone or clay.

kneading: squeezing clay to make it smooth and remove air bubbles.

layout: the way **text** and pictures are arranged on a page.

loading (a pen): filling it with ink, usually with a small brush.

logo: specially designed symbol or trademark for a company, product or person.

lower-case letter: small letter or **minuscule.**

majuscule: **capital** or **upper-case letter**.

margin: area of space around a piece of writing.

minuscule: small or **lower-case letter.**

portfolio: flat case for carrying artwork. Also the work inside.

resist: method using two substances that do not mix, such as wax and watercolor paint or masking fluid and gouache paint.

round letter: letter which closely follows the shape of the letter 'o'.

rubbing: the mark or impression left by rubbing wax crayon or a soft pencil over a sheet of paper laid over some **incised** or raised letters.

ruling up: measuring and drawing **guidelines** to write some calligraphy.

sans serif: a letter without **serifs**.

serif: small **stroke** which is added to the beginning and end of some letter **strokes**.

skeleton letter: letter written in its most basic form, with a thin nib or writing tool.

stem: main vertical **stroke** of a letter.

stencil: sheet from which shapes or letters have been cut out. Color is applied through gaps onto the surface underneath to reproduce the cut-out shapes.

stroke: part of a letter made by a single pen stroke.

text: writing.

thumbnail: small, rough sketch of a **layout**.

typeface: style of type in printing.

upper-case letter: capital letter or majuscule.

wash: watered-down paint brushed over paper.

weight: relationship between a letter's height (**x-height** for **minuscules**) and the thickness of the nib it is written with.

writing-line: line on which letters are written. Also called the **base line**.

x-height: height of the main **body** of a **minuscule**.

Useful information

If you want to take calligraphy further, there is information you might find useful on this page.

Making a portfolio

A portfolio for carrying your work, as shown on page 39, can be quite expensive. Here's how to make a simple one from sheets of cardboard.

You will need:

Three sheets of stiff cardboard

A sheet of stiff paper   Some ribbon

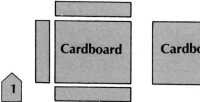

Cut two sheets of the cardboard to the size you need your portfolio to be. Cut three flaps to fit the sides out of the third sheet.

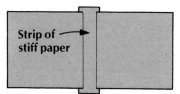

Glue the two sheets to each side of a strip of stiff paper, as shown here. This will act as a hinge for the portfolio.

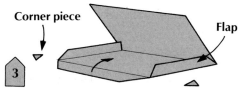

Glue the flaps to the sides of one sheet of card. Cut off their corners and fold them inwards.

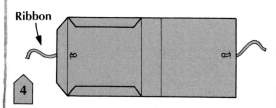

Slit the cardboard where shown here. Thread ribbon through each slit, gluing about ⅕ inch of one end to the cardboard.

Books to read

General

Pen lettering – Ann Camp (A & C Black).

The Calligrapher's Project Book – Susanne Haines (Collins).

The Complete Guide to Calligraphy – (Phaidon Press).

Lettering and Typography – Tony Potter (Usborne).

The Calligrapher's Handbook – Ed. Heather Child. (A & C Black).

Writing and Illumination and Lettering – Edward Johnston (A & C Black).

Advanced Calligraphy Techniques – Diana Hoare (Chartwell)

History

Historical scripts – Stan Knight (A & C Black).

The story of writing – Donald Jackson. (Barrie & Jenkins).

A book of scripts – Alfred Fairbank (Faber)

Special techniques

Quill-cutting – see Donald Jackson's piece in **The Calligrapher's Handbook** (A & C Black).

Creative lettering: drawing and design – Michael Harvey (Bodley Head).

Painting for calligraphers – Marie Angel (Pelham Books).

Carving letters in stone and wood – Michael Harvey (Bodley Head).

Chinese Brush Painting – Jane Evans (Collins).

Handwriting

The Irene Wellington Copy Book – Irene Wellington (A & C Black).

Compilations

Calligraphy Today – Heather Child (A & C Black).

Contemporary Calligraphy – (Trefoil Books).

Treasury of Alphabets and Lettering – Jan Tschichold (Omega).

Specialized calligraphy

If you are interested in learning Chinese, Hebrew or Islamic calligraphy, here are some books to start with.

Chinese Calligraphy – Yee Chiang (Methuen).

Hebrew Calligraphy – Jay Seth Greenspan (Schocken Books).

Islamic Calligraphy – Yasin Hamid Safadi (Thames and Hudson).

Societies

Several countries have societies for calligraphers. They will send you information on courses.

USA

Washington Calligraphers Guild, Box 3688, Merrifield, VA 22116

Society of Scribes Ltd, Box 933, New York, NY 10150

Society for Calligraphy, Box 64174, Los Angeles, CA 90064

Canada

Bow Valley Calligraphy Guild, P.O. Box 1647, Station M, Calgary, Alberta T2P 2L7.

La Société des Calligraphes, P.O. Box 704, Snowdon, Montreal, Québec H3X 3X8.

Index

First published in 1990. Usborne Publishing Ltd, Usborne House,
83-85 Saffron Hill, London, EC1N 8RT, England. Copyright ©1990 Usborne Publishing Limited.